Abyssinian Cats

The Ultimate Pet Guide for Abyssinian Cats

Abyssinian Cat General Info, Purchasing, Care, Cost, Keeping, Health, Supplies, Food, Breeding and More Included!

By Lolly Brown

Copyrights and Trademarks

Disclaimer and Legal Notice

Foreword

Abyssinian cats are not just irresistibly cuddly, they're also witty and intelligent creatures but it may not be the right choice for everyone. Before you decide whether or not it might be the right breed for you and your family, you need to enough gather information, and invest your time and effort in getting to know this cat breed.

Aside from the general information, biological background, and physical attributes of Abyssinian cats, this book will also delve deeper on how to take care of Abyssinian cats in terms of it health, nutrition, grooming, habitat and maintenance.

Table of Contents

Introduction

The Abyssinian is considered as one of the oldest of all breeds and domestic cats. According to most historians, they resemble a sculptural and painted representation of Ancient Egyptian cats. These cats are also active, social and very vocal! They bond very close with the family, or their owners and they wanted to be involved in everything that their owners do.

Another great thing about Abyssinian cats is that they can adapt to any environment, so acquiring them as a pet will just take a short time for them to get used to their new home. They are easy to train because they're naturally intelligent creatures. In fact, they're quite good at training their owners on how or where to pet them. Abyssinians are not your ordinary lap cats but they love hugs and kisses (I mean who doesn't right?). They're also very sweet and caring to their owners, which is why they're perfect as family pets.

They are smart, witty, active and fun cats to be with but like any other pets, these creatures can be demanding in terms of attention and respect! Before you bring an Abyssinian home, however, you should be a responsible cat owner, and learn everything you can about this breed and how to care for it properly.

Aside from the general information, biological background, and physical attributes of Abyssinian cats, this book will also delve deeper on how to take care of Abyssinian cats in terms of it health, nutrition, grooming, habitat and maintenance. You will also be informed about how to breed them, and the criteria for showing. Pros and cons will also be provided as well as some links to resources that can help you to better understand this awesome breed.

We hope this book will be of great help to you as a newbie, or even for those who have experienced taking care of cats already. It doesn't hurt to learn new things so read on!

Chapter One: Biological Information

Abyssinian cats are not just irresistibly cuddly, they're also witty and intelligent creatures but it may not be the right choice for everyone. Before you decide whether or not it might be the right breed for you and your family, you need to enough gather information, and invest your time and effort in getting to know this cat breed.

In this chapter you will receive an introduction to the breed including some basic biological facts and general information as well as the history of how it came about. This information, in combination with the practical information about keeping in the next chapter, will help you decide if this is the perfect companion for you.

Taxonomy, Origin and History

The Abyssinian cats have a scientific name of *Felis domesticus*. They belong in Kingdom *Animalia*, Phylum *Chordata*, Class *Mammalia*, Order *Carnivora*, Family *Felidae*, Genus *Felis*, and Species *Domesticus*.

As mentioned earlier, Abyssinian cats are originally from Abyssinia, now known as Ethiopia. They were believed to be one of the of most ancient cat breeds because their existence dates back to many centuries ago during the time of the early Egyptians. They were the companions or pets of Egyptian gods and/or Pharaohs.

These cats have originated from Egypt (particularly around the Nile Valley) but it was further developed in United Kingdom. Around 1860's, Lord Robert Napier brought back home an Abyssinian cat from his military expedition named "Zula" or "Zulu." It was the name of the first Abyssinian cat recorded in history, and it is also believed to be the direct descendent of a sacred Egyptian cat called *Bastet*.

Zula's coat has a ticking pattern in it similar to the coat of wild rabbits, and because of that is has alternative names like Bunny Cat or Hare Cat.

People got interested in the cat's amazing coat and physical attributes; eventually Zula was randomly bred to other similar looking cat breeds which resulted in the Abyssinian breed we now see today.

The breed became very popular, and was soon brought to other parts of the world including the United States, Europe, Asia and Canada. However, because of the devastation brought about by the two World Wars, the Abyssinian breeds decreased in production, fortunately new breeds were saved, and imported to other countries.

Around 1960's, the feline leukemia virus almost threatened the breed's population again in Great Britain, but breeding was eventually re-established, and continued to flourish until today.

The Abyssinian cats are now a member of several cat organizations all over the world such as the Cat Fanciers' Association (CFA), Fédération Internationale Féline (FIFe), The International Cat Association (TICA), Australian Cat Federation (ACF), Canadian Cat Association (CCA – AFC) and many others.

Other names for Abyssinian cats are the following:

- Ticked Cat
- British Tick Cat
- Bunny Cat
- Rabbit Cat

- Hare Cat
- Aby Cat

Size, Life Span, and Physical Appearance

Abyssinian cats are medium – size cats that weigh an average of 8 – 12 pounds for both male and female species. It stands at about 2 ft. or 60 cm and can live up to 15 – 20 years or more depending on how you take care of its health.

These cats have quite a muscular body with long and arched necks. It also possess a relatively large and alert ears, has long legs, and its eyes are almond – shaped usually gold/yellowish, and green, though sometimes they also have bluish eye colors.

Abyssinian cats have many coat color variations such as lavender or lilac, chocolate, black, silver, blue, fawn (pale tan), cinnamon, ruddy (bluish – gray), and dark brown. One of their unique physical characteristics is the ticking of individual hairs on their coat, and gives it a sort of mottled appearance. It is also soft, fine, smooth and silky.

Abyssinian cats also have a broad head, slender physique, and short tail. They're the most ancient looking cats in today's modern domestic breeds. Their rich history of being once called as the "Child of the Gods" as well as their great attitude made them popular among cat enthusiasts.

Quick Facts

Origin: Egypt, Ethiopia

Pedigree: descendants of Bastet ancient cat breed

Breed Size: medium – size breed

Body Type and Appearance: Has a muscular yet slender type body with long legs, sharp eyes, large ears, short tail and broad head.

Group: Cat Fanciers' Association (CFA), Fédération Internationale Féline (FIFe), The International Cat Association (TICA), Australian Cat Federation (ACF), Canadian Cat Association (CCA – AFC).

Height: 2 ft. or 60 cm

Weight: average of 8 – 12 pounds

Coat Length: short ticked coat

Coat Texture: fine, silky, smooth, soft

Color: lavender or lilac, chocolate, black, silver, blue, fawn (pale tan), cinnamon, ruddy (bluish – gray), and dark brown

Temperament: witty, friendly, active sociable, and affectionate

Strangers: friendly around strangers

Other Cats: generally good with other cat breeds if properly introduced, trained, and socialized

Other Pets: friendly with other pets such as cat-friendly dogs but if not properly introduce may result to potential aggression

Training: clever, responsive, and very trainable

Exercise Needs: provide toys for mental and physical stimulation

Health Conditions: generally healthy but predisposed to common illnesses such as Dental Diseases, Atopy, Arthritis, Kidney Diseases, Hypertension, Heart Diseases, Feline Aortic Thromboembolism (FATE), Congestive Heart Failure, Hyperthyroidism, Diabetes, Feline Lower Urinary Tract Disease (FLUTD), Kidney Failure

Lifespan: average 15 to 20 years

Chapter Two: Abyssinian Cats as Pets

Now that you have learned general information about Abyssinian cats, their historical background, their physical characteristics, and how they were once deemed as sacred cats that Egyptians were worshipping back then, it's now time to know if these pets are suited for your or your family.

In this chapter, you will get a whole lot of information on its pros and cons, some legal requirements in keeping one, how they deal with other pets, its personalities and behaviors, and what makes it a great pet.

What Makes It a Great Pet

If you are planning to acquire an Abyssinian cat as your pet, it's important that your personality and that of your cat is a match so that you can enjoy their company and vice – versa. In this section you'll be given an overview on their behavioral characteristics or temperament, the cost of owning one as well as how you can socialize or introduce them to your other pets if any.

Temperament and Behavioral Characteristics

As mentioned in the previous chapter, the Abysinnian breed is an intelligent, witty, fun, and affectionate breed. They are mostly active but can still be quite docile or prim and proper. They possess a swift and finesse attitude that certainly matches that elegant ancient look.

Abyssinian cats can also be hyper at times because they are naturally good hunters as what most cats are. It may be hard for you as their owner to make them sit still because they are also energetic which is why training at a young age is highly recommended. They are obedient and loyal pets with a very caring attitude.

If you want to get along with this cat breed, you have to make sure that you give them respect and enough attention not just to their basic needs but as their companion as well. Keep in mind that just like any other animals, they need sufficient affection from their owners so that they can grow fondly of you and perhaps form a strong bond with the family.

These cats are also perfect for children particularly those who are around 6 – 8 years old as long as they will be treating the cats politely and with respect; he's also smart to stay away from toddlers. They are highly and naturally sociable, and they also love to interact with humans.

Behavioral Characteristics with other Pets

These types of cats are also friendly with other household pets such as dogs, other cat breeds, rabbits, guinea pigs and the likes. They will happily play with a Golden Retriever or any other pets as long as they are properly introduced and socialized. Socializing cats at an early age with other pets will make it easier for them to bond, interact, and live with one another. These cats also like to play with pets who are a match for its energy and curiosity. Abyssinian cats are also known to get along with large parrots or other birds.

These cats are also quite fearless to other animals as long as it will not cause them any trouble like territorial dispute or during feeding time, although of course to prevent this you need to make sure that all of your pets gets enough space, has enough food and more than an adequate living condition.

Pros and Cons of Abyssinian Cats

Pros

- They are smart, loyal, obedient, curious, active, and fun cats They can be easily trained, and very affectionate
- Has a variety of coating and patterns; their coat is ticked and very soft and smooth.
- Gets along with other cats or pets especially dogs and other cat breeds, if properly socialized and introduced.
- A family companion, these cats are perfect for children and people in general; love to hang out with its owners.

Cons

- Not the usual lap cat
- Nutrition should be taken care of, to avoid suffering from obesity; can be prone to certain genetic conditions
- Naturally active and curious which sometimes can lead to trouble if not properly trained.
- Does not do well in isolation, demands lots of attention.

- Keeping them can be quite costly because supplies need to be bought all the time, and possible medical or vet expenses.
- Generally low maintenance but things such as toys, grooming, and food may need to always be replaced or replenished on a constant basis.

Legal Requirements and Cat Licensing

If you are planning to acquire a cat as your pet, there are certain restrictions and regulations that you need to be aware of. Licensing requirements for pets varies in different countries, regions, and states.

In the United States there are no federal requirements for licensing either cats or even dogs – these rules are regulated at the state level. While it is true that most states do not have a mandatory requirement for people to license their cats, it is always a good idea to do so because it will not only serve as protection for your pet but also for you.

Here are some things you need to know regarding the acquirement of Abyssinian cats both in United States and in United Kingdom.

United States Licensing for Cats

The average annual license cost is $10.00 or more (costs may vary depending on the state where you live). Cat licenses for senior citizens are $5.00, so if you want to save a few bucks, better let your grannies license your cat for you.

When you acquire license for your cat you will be given a cat number that can then be linked to your contact information. If your cat gets lost and someone finds it, its license can be used to track you down so that they'll be able to return to you your pet. Of course, this information will only be available if your cat wears a collar with an ID tag.

It is also ideal that four month old cats and up as well as indoor cats such as Abyssinians should still have a license because it is required by municipal law. Even those cats that never leave the house have a way of getting out through accidentally open doors, gates, or windows. These cat breed is particularly intelligent and can outsmart you.

A natural disaster may cause your pet to run the safety of your house therefore having your cat licensed will make you easily find your pet if in case he/she gets lost.

If you want to apply for a cat license, you can search the website of your municipal or state government online. You will be able to download the application form, and just follow the procedure. After filling up the form, you can mail it to their office together with a fee. Although, in some states there is currently no fee for a cat license so make sure to check first and find out how much it cost.

Documentary requirements must be submitted before permanently getting a pet license such as current rabies certificate, spay and neuter proof, and microchip (further discussion later).

In most states, these are the main documents needed to get a cat license, although, there might be additional requirements that need to be submitted in other states. The temporary license will be considered only as temporary until you have provided all the necessary requirements.

If you don't want to put a collar on your cat, a good alternative option is to have him/her micro-chipped. A microchip serves the same function but they can be embedded under your cat's skin so that it won't be lost. The procedure for having your cat micro-chipped is very quick and painless.

United Kingdom Licensing for Cats

In United Kingdom, there are no overarching licensing requirements for cats but you will need to get a special permit if you plan to travel with your cat into or out of the country.

Your cat may also be subject to a quarantine period to

make sure he isn't carrying a disease like rabies because rabies has been eradicated in UK for a long time through safety measures like these, which is why it is important for the country to maintain this kind of status.

Licensing for Cats in Other Countries

If you are planning to travel with your cat or bring them to other countries other than the U.S. and the U.K., you may need to bring proper documents such as your state permit for your cat, rabies or vaccinations certificate, and current health condition to ensure that there'll be no transfer of virus or diseases to the country you wish to go to with your pet. Aside from that, there could be other requirements so be sure to check first the country laws regarding bringing of pets or travelling with them in other nations.

Cost of Owning a Cat

In this section you will receive an overview of the expenses associated with purchasing and keeping cats as pets such as food and treats, grooming and cleaning supplies, toys, veterinary care, and other costs so that you can prepare for it ahead of time.

Are You Financially Prepared?

Keeping pets in general can be costly, and even if these cats are low maintenance and quite inexpensive compared to other breed, you will still need to provide its supplies to maintain a healthy lifestyle and adequate environment for your pet.

These things will definitely add up to your daily budget, and the cost will vary depending on where you buy it; the brand of the accessories, the nutrients included in its food, the time being etc. If you want to seriously own an Abyssinian cat as a pet you should be able to cover the necessary costs it entails.

The initial expenses associated with keeping Manx as pets include the cost of the cat itself as well as the its bed, accessories, toys, initial vaccinations, micro- chipping or licensing, spay/neuter surgery as well as grooming supplies.

Average Price of Abyssinians Cats

The average price for an Abyssinian cat kitten with a desired coat color or show quality ranges from $900 - $1,200, while low quality cats from backyard breeders can cost just about $300 - $500 or more. Of course, it can become more expensive, especially if it is from a reputable breeder or sometimes it depends on the cat's age, the vaccines/surgery included as well as the overall grooming of the cat.

Keep in mind that the cost highly depends on the quality of the breed; the rarer the color pattern, the more expensive it can be. There could also be additional charges if your pet will be shipped, it can add up to the price of your kitten to some extent. In some stores, it may also require a $250 deposit, so be prepared to have the money if you already decided to buy an Abyssinian cat.

Other Essentials

Aside from the purchase price you also need to buy other things like bed, dishes, toys, grooming and food supplies. You also need to set aside enough budget for vaccinations especially for kittens, as well as various expenses like license renewal, spay/neuter procedures, microchipping, vet consultations, and other needed accessories (especially if you will show your cat at competitions).

Abyssinian cats are generally medium – size cats which is why a normal sized cat bed or even a large size one is best for your pet. Generally, the average cost for a normal size cat bed starts at around $40 - $50. In addition to providing your Abyssinian cats with a cat bed, you should also make sure that it has a set of high-quality food and water bowls or dishes.

The best materials for these are stainless steel because it is easy to clean, cannot be easily chewed or eaten and won't acquire bacteria, another good option is ceramic. The average cost for a quality set of stainless steel bowls is about $30.

Since Abyssinian cats are naturally active and playful, you need to provide them with plenty of stimulation to keep their intelligent and curious minds entertained. It's highly recommended that you buy an assortment of toys for your cat until you learn what kind it prefers. Minimum cost of toys is approximately $20 or more, cost may vary depending on the brand.

Feeding your Abyssinian cats a healthy diet is very important for its health and wellness, especially for a very active pet. A high-quality diet for cats is not cheap especially for a medium- sized breed like the Abyssinian. The right amount of nutrients should be provided to maintain its healthy and exotic – looking physique. You should set aside around $50 for a high-quality cat food which will last you about a month. You should also include a monthly budget of at least $10 for treats so you can reward during training.

There will be times that you may need to let your Abyssinian cat play outside the house or even present it for a show, that's why you might need several cat accessories like a leash (if you're planning to train them or walk them outside), and other things like cat costumes or dresses, grooming materials as well as any shelter repairs for your cat. On average, extra accessories may cause at least $50 depending on brand and quality of the product. In addition to all of these you should plan for occasional extra costs like replacements for worn-out toys, cleaning products and license renewal.

Medical Expenses

Medical expenses such as micro-chipping, initial vaccinations for kittens, spay/neuter surgery, and the occasional vet consultations should also be considered as part of your budget for your pet.

Micro-chipping

In the United States and United Kingdom there are no federal or state requirements saying that you have to have your cat micro-chipped, but it is very ideal, as mentioned earlier, your Abyssinian could slip outside through an open door or window without you noticing it.

If someone finds it without identification, they can take it to a shelter to have its microchip scanned. A microchip is something that is implanted under your cat's skin and it carries a number that is linked to your contact information. The procedure takes just a few minutes to perform and it only costs about $50 on average, but in some states cost may vary and there are certain documents that you may need to submit in your local government.

Initial Vaccinations

This is only applicable if you acquire a kitten; during your kitten's first year of life, it will require a number of different vaccinations. If you purchase your kitten from a reputable breeder, it might already have had a few but you'll still need more over the next few months as well as booster shots each year.

Abyssinian cats can still be prone to common viral and bacterial infections, however, emergencies may arise anytime so just to be safe you may need to provide these vaccinations to prevent common cat viruses such as panleukopenia, calicivirus, rabies and rhinotracheitis, to name a few.

Also if your cat have the appropriate boosters they need, at a young age, it can definitely lengthen their life expectancy. You should include it in your budget which may cost at around $50 or more.

Spay/Neuter Surgery

If you don't plan to breed your cats you should have it neutered (for males) or spayed (for females) before 6 months of age.

Spaying and neutering is a kind of procedure that removes your pet's reproductive system so that won't have any unwanted pregnancies.

Spaying or neutering your pet decreases the likelihood of certain types of cancers and eliminates the possibility of your pet producing an unwanted offspring. The cost for this surgery will vary depending where you go and on the gender of your cat.

If you go to a traditional veterinary surgeon, the cost for spay/neuter surgery could be very high but you can save money by going to a veterinary clinic. The average cost for neuter surgery is $50 to $100 and spay surgery costs about $100 to $200.

Veterinary Consultations

As mentioned earlier, Abyssinian kittens may get ill due to viral and bacterial infection, that's why you may need to take them to a vet for a medical check-up every now and then.

In order to keep your cat healthy, you should take it to the veterinarian about every six months after it passes kitten-hood. You might have to take it more often for the first 12 months to make sure he gets his vaccines on time.

The average cost for a vet visit is about $40. If in case, your cat get sick, it's better and wiser to set aside a portion of your budget for any medical needs that will come up.

Chapter Three: Purchasing and Selecting a Healthy Breed

In this chapter you will be provided with the criteria on selecting a healthy Abyssinian cat breed as well as a reputable and trustworthy breeder. You will also learn where to purchase an Abyssinian cat breed, and you can also check out the links provided in this chapter if you wanted to purchase a cat online or if you need information on where to visit a particular cat breeder. It's essential that before you purchase any cat for this matter, you should first consider on who takes care of them and how they are being taken care of, especially if they're still kittens. If you find a reputable breeder you can be sure to acquire a good cat breed.

Where to Purchase an Abyssinian Cat Breed

There are many places where you can buy an Abyssinian cat. In this section, you will learn its advantages and possibly some disadvantages. Compare one from the other and see for yourself which could be suited for you.

Local Pet Stores

The first place that everyone goes to when buying cats, or any animal for that matter is of course, a pet store. However, some local pet stores may not have an Abyssinian breed since this is quite a special kind of cat. And although their prevalence is common, Abyssinian cat may still not be available. Another disadvantage of buying in pet stores is that you don't know where the breed comes from or how they were raised, and even if you ask the employees working in that pet store they may not have an idea about it. According to many breeders, pet stores are mostly not properly taking care of such pets, which is why you should not try and rescue these pets by buying them, because they will just be re-stock by these pet stores.

As for the advantages, pet stores are locally available in most areas, they're easy to purchase, and they can also be delivered to your home if it is just near your area of residence, just make sure that it is a reputable pet shop.

Backyard/Private Breeders

Your best option is buying from backyard or private breeders or local breeders. You can find them online, or through a referral from a friend or relative. The reason why this is your best bet is because you can easily determine if they are reputable or not since they're the ones who bred or has taken care of the kittens from the beginning. You can also do a bargain with them, and even get some tips on how to take care of the breed. The only major disadvantage is that you have to go personally to visit the place where these animals are bred, or if you decide to purchase them already, you have to pick them up yourself. If they are far from your area, it may not be advisable, plus you could also waste your time and money if you found out that they're not a reputable breeder or if their pets are not healthy.

Online Stores

You can also buy cats that are posted online from private advertisers in pet websites. However, it'll be hard for you to determine if the cat is healthy or not if you just check its photos or videos provided by the seller. You may need to still visit the breeder to personally check the Abyssinian cat that they are selling. You can join forums online so that you can get personal recommendations on where to buy a breed.

Cat Conventions or Pet Conferences

You can purchase from pet conferences or cat conventions (if any) that is near your area. This is a great place to buy because people who attend these kinds of events are cat enthusiasts, and legit breeders. You can also be sure of the breed's quality as well as the vaccination papers and/or proper licensing requirements. Another advantage is that you'll also get to meet other cat breeders and pet owners.

Characteristics of a Reputable Breeder

Now that you already know where to purchase your cat, it's time to determine who to buy it from. Selecting a breeder is the first step before you buy any pet because if the breeder is reputable, caring, and a responsible caregiver, you can be sure that the cats or breeds is well – taken care of. Here are the following guidelines for you to be able to choose a reputable cat breeder:

- Visit the website for each breeder on your list (if they have one) and look for key information about the breeder's history and experience.

- Check for CFA or TICA registrations and a license, if they have any.
- If the website doesn't provide any information about the facilities or the breeder, you shouldn't waste your time with them.
- Ask the breeder questions about his experience with breeding cats in general and about the Abyssinian cat you are looking for.
- Ask for information about the breeding stock including registration numbers and health information.
- Expect a reputable breeder to ask you questions about yourself as well. A responsible breeder wants to make sure that his cats go to good homes.
- Ask for a tour of the facilities, including the place where the pets are kept as well as the facilities housing the kittens/cats.
- If things look unorganized or unclean, do not purchase from the breeder.
- Make sure the breeding stock is in good condition and that the kittens are all healthy-looking and active.
- Make sure the breeder provides some kind of health guarantee and ask about any vaccinations the kittens/cats may already have. Put down a deposit, if needed to reserve a kitten if they aren't ready to come home yet.

- Ask the breeder to give you a tour of the facilities. Make sure the facilities where the kittens/cats are housed is clean and sanitary. But if there is evidence of diarrhea, do not purchase from that breeder because the other cats may already be sick or infected.

Characteristics of a Healthy Breed

After determining where to buy, and who to buy from, the next step is the most important and fun part! It's time to choose your very own Abyssinian cat or kitten! Since you have already determined that the remaining breeders on your list are responsible and reputable, you now have to make sure that the Abyssinian kittens or cats that they have are healthy not just physically but also behaviorally, and of course, if he/she is match to your personality.

Here are the characteristics to keep in mind when selecting a healthy Abyssinian cat breed:

Check the Cat's Physique

- Examine the cat's or kitten's body for any signs of illness and potential injuries.
- Check the skin and/or coat color
- Check its body parts

- The kitten/s should have clear, bright eyes with no discharge.
- The kitten/s ears should be clean, and clear with no discharge or inflammation.
- The kitten/s stomach shouldn't be distended or swollen.
- The kitten/s stomach should be able to walk and run normally without any mobility problems.
- Make sure that its teeth and gums are also in good condition
- Avoid any cats that look lethargic and those that have difficulty moving because they could be sick.

Check the Cat's Behavior

- The kitten/s should be active, and playful, interacting with each other in a healthy way.
- Try to observe the litter as a whole, and watch how the cats interact with each other so you can determine their personalities.
- You can also pet them or play with them to see how they interact with humans.
- Try picking them up to see if they are frightened to human contact or not, if they are too scared, it could mean that they are not properly socialized.
- If all the cats are in good condition, and seems to like you, that's a good sign that your breeder is also

reputable. All you have to do now is to choose who best connects with you.

List of Breeders and Rescue Websites

There are so many Abyssinian cat breeders to choose from, that's why you need to do some research and decide which reputable breeder you should buy from before you start purchasing kittens.

If you want a kitten, your best chance is to find a local Abyssinian breeder. But before you do, consider first whether adopting an adult cat might be a better option for you. There are plenty of adult Abyssinian cats out there who have been abandoned by their previous owners, and they are looking for a new home. When you adopt a cat or kitten you are actually saving a life. Adopting a cat can sometimes be cheaper than buying from a breeder and in many cases you can already get a cage and some accessories that comes with adopting these abandoned cats. Many adult cats ready for adoption have also already been spayed or neutered, litter trained, and are already caught up on vaccinations so adopting a cat is not just a good thing to do, it's also economical.

Here is the list of breeders and adoption rescue websites around United States and United Kingdom:

United States Breeders and Rescue Websites

The International Cat Association (TICA)
<http://www.tica.org/find-a-breeder/item/189-abyssinian-breeders>

Fanciers Breeder Referral List
<http://www.breedlist.com/breeders/aby_np.html>

Kahali Cattery
<https://www.kahalicats.com/>

Abytopia
<http://www.abytopia.com/>

Aksum Abyssinians
<http://aksumabyssinians.com/kittens.html>

Alexy Abyssinians
<http://www.angelfire.com/nc2/alexyabys/index.html>

Pets 4 You
<https://www.pets4you.com/abyssinian.html>

Abyssinian Breed Council

<http://www.abyssinianbc.org/>

Breeding – Cats

<http://www.breeding-cats.com/abyssinian-cat-breeders.html#United_States>

Front Range Abyssinians Somalis

<http://www.frontrangeabyssinianssomalis.com/Available.html>

Red Ferne Abyssinians

<http://www.redferneabyssinians.com/kittens.htm >

Southern California Abyssinian Rescue

<http://www.socaabyrescue.com/>

Adopt – a – Pet

<http://www.adoptapet.com/s/abyssinian-cats-for-adoption>

Pet Finder

<https://www.petfinder.com/cat-breeds/Abyssinian>

Pure Bred Cat Rescue

<http://purebredcatrescue.org/choosing-the-right-breed/abyssinians-somalis/>

Anygma Abyssinians

<http://www.anyabys.net/adopt-a-homeless-aby.html>

United Kingdom Breeders and Rescue Websites

Pets 4 Homes UK

<https://www.pets4homes.co.uk/sale/cats/abyssinian/>

Abyssinian Cat Club

<http://www.abyssiniancatclub.com/breeders.html>

Koperkat Abyssinians

<http://koperkatabyssinians.co.uk/>

Abyssinian Association UK

 <http://www.abycatassociation.co.uk/>

Abderus Abyssinians

<http://www.abderus.co.uk/>

Melisani Abyssinians

<http://www.abyssinian-cat.co.uk/ >

Surfin Abyssinians & Somalis

<http://www.surfinabyssinians.co.uk/>

CrystalPaws Abyssinians

<http://www.crystalcats.co.uk/ >

Chapter Four: Habitat Requirements for Abyssinian Cats

Now that you have already bought an Abyssinian cat, it's time to learn how to maintain them and set up a great environment so they can happily grow with you or your family. In this chapter you will learn the basics about your cat's habitat requirements including its shelter, and useful accessories needed. You will also learn some tips on how to cat - proof your house before your new pet arrives as well as some guidelines on how you can maintain an adequate living condition for them.

Housing Requirements

As with most cats, your Abyssinian will need enough space to roam around with, and also cat bed or a shelter to relax in after a whole day of fun and games.

Cat Bed vs. Shelter/Cages

As mentioned earlier, you have to buy a cat bed that is big enough for your kitten or cat. The bigger the bed, the better for your pet! If you bought a relatively large cat bed even if your pet is still a kitten, it can be both comfortable for them and also economic for you because as they grow larger over time, you won't have to buy a bigger bed anymore. Make it more comfortable by providing bed sheets or even a small pillow; just be sure that it is a disposable pillow because it can potentially be ruined by your cats.

According to some owners, there are some cats that prefers to sleep on the floor, on a box or somewhere else, if that's the kind of pet you have, then just let them be especially if it is their first time on your house or with a new owner. They may still be adjusting to their new environment, so don't force them to immediately sleep on the cat bed you bought. However, to encourage your cat to use the bed, try sprinkling it with catnip. You may even want to keep several beds around the house in places your Abyssinian is likely to hang out like in a quiet room, under a window or in the living room.

If you want to buy a cage for your pet, it's again better to buy a bigger one so that you won't have to buy every time your pet grows larger. Buying a shelter for your pet is entirely up to you, but your Abyssinian cat may not like to stay there all the time since it's an affectionate breed, and it is the kind of cat that likes to hang around with people.

The major disadvantage of buying a shelter for your cat is that you have to be able to clean it every now and then so that it won't become dusty or accumulate any unwanted creatures like ants, unlike if you're just going to buy a cat bed, it'll be easy to just wash it or bring it to the laundry shop. However, it may be best to purchase a shelter for them if you have other pets like dogs or other cat breeds so that they won't fight over territories especially if you only live in an apartment.

Play Pen, Perches, Toys and Other Accessories

If you don't want to let your cat run loose in the house, you should provide an exercise pen in addition to its cage or cat bed. Abyssinian cats are active creatures and they are also naturally curious, so if you don't want them roaming around the house and sniffing your stuff, you may want to give them their own play space that has toys and interesting stuff to get their attention off of kitchen supplies or your house figurines.

Aside from that you may want to also provide your Abyssinian cat with a perch or a cat tree since cats love to climb. You can also install shelving on your walls to give your cat a place to perch, so that he/she can have an overview of the whole place and feel secure. Just be careful about decorating your house with things that can be knocked over; cats are notorious for making a game of knocking things off shelves.

Your Abyssinian cats will also need plenty of stimulating and engaging toys to play with to help him work off its excess energy. As with most cats, Abyssinians are also naturally an athletic and agile animal which is why playing or exercising is essential to make them be mentally and physically stimulated. Playing also serves as an outlet for their natural hunting drive, and it's also a chance for them to bond with you. It's both fun and healthy for your pet.

Cats in general are very good at keeping themselves busy, you don't need to buy expensive toys in order to keep them stimulated, although sometimes it is also advisable because some toys are designed to develop certain physical aspects.

Aside from toys available in pet stores, here are some examples of improvised or DIY toys you can find in your household to make your cat or kitten active and lively! You can be as creative and interactive as you want to be when making activities with these things like ping pong balls or golf balls, flashlights (cats are crazy for it), paper bags, empty cardboard boxes, dangling Objects, other various stuff toys. However, before using such items, you have to make sure that you remove any objects that your cat could chew or swallow such as ribbons, plastic bag, feathers, rubber bands, strings, paper clips, pins, tinsel, needles or other small decorations. If possible, always supervise your cat when he/she is playing and keep harmful objects out of reach.

Housing Temperature

Another environmental factor you need to consider for your cats is the temperature. Even if these cats have furry coats that keep them warm, the ambient temperature in your house should still be at a normal range, not too hot and not too cold either. You should also avoid exposing your cat to too much sunlight because it might cause skin or coat issues.

Guidelines on How to Keep Your Cat Happy and Safe

If you are still waiting for your pet to arrive, it's the perfect time to prepare your home (and yourself) so that they can be protected from various household hazards and be able to eliminate any unwanted accidents or situations. Below are some guidelines on how to cat – proof your home and how to keep them happy as well.

- Provide fences, a screened porch or a safe enclosure. Be sure to cat-proof your yard so that your cat could experience the outdoors safely.
- Remove any poisonous plants since cats like to chew anything. If your cat chew any plants, even the non-poisonous ones can cause vomiting and diarrhea.
- Install padded perches indoors near a window frame or in your patio so that your pet could enjoy and hang out and do not leave your doors and screens Unlocked, they may slip out (and they will) so don't leave them unattended.
- Do not leave your appliances plugged, as mentioned earlier, they will chew anything including electric wires, not only is this potentially fatal for your cat but also a dangerous threat for your home.
- Buy a harness and train your cat to walk on a leash when going around the neighborhood.

- Consider buying a ready-made cat tree to provide climbing opportunities for your cat inside.
- Plant cat grass inside your house where your cat can graze.
- Make sure to keep lots of cat toys out and put anything precious and destructible away.
- Make sure to keep away toxic liquids or materials like cleaning supplies or other household items that can harm them.
- Make sure that your cat/kitten will not be able to enter bathrooms or kitchens alone because it can be dangerous for them. Always supervise and keep an eye on them or better yet lock the doors so that they can't easily enter.

Chapter Five: Nutrition and Feeding

Proper nutrition will go a long way for your cat's health and growth. Feeding your Abyssinian cat is not that complicated but you have to make sure that its level of activity, age, and weight should be taken into consideration to meet its nutritional diet needs. Abyssinian cats should be given the right amount of recommended food for a balanced nutrition because proper diet can lengthen the life expectancy of your cat and also protect them from serious illnesses.

In this section, you'll learn the majority of your pet's nutritional needs as well as some feeding guidelines, foods that are good and harmful for your cat, and also a review of the brand of cat foods ideal for Abyssinians.

Nutritional Needs of Abyssinian Cats

As with most cats, Abyssinians are natural predators. These creatures are programmed to hunt, catch, kill, and then eat whatever they killed. Even if your pet is a domestic cat, he/she cannot deny his/her true nature. When it comes to feeding cats only eat one thing: meat. If you don't give them meat (beef, pork, chicken, fish etc.) or formulated meat products (canned cat foods) you will have a hard time feeding them because they will reject whatever you're offering that is not a meat.

Abyssinian cats share ancestry with some of the animal kingdom's most powerful felines such as lions, tigers, and cheetahs, so whenever you are feeding them, keep in mind that their relatives are not seen eating apples, or grass or drinking milk (although kittens love them). Some owners feed their cats with these kinds of food which is both absurd and inappropriate. As with most mammals, cats are carnivores so be sure to keep that in mind.

If you're a vegetarian or if you're trying to slim down your cat, feeding them with vegetables is not the right way of doing that. They're not omnivores like humans that can switch from one food type to another. So don't feed your cats foods like grains, or fruits or whatnot. You may offer it to them as a treat but not as a primary meal.

Abyssinian cats must be given eat protein – rich foods as well as some healthy fats as part of their diet. You should not feed your Abyssinian cat with too much carbs (a small amount can be beneficial but make sure you're giving the right amount) because their digestive system can't process it well. Too much carbs can lead to extreme obesity which can also develop into diabetes – it's one of the most common diseases suffered by cats nowadays because of improper diet.

What is Free – Feeding?

There's a new trend online that suggests free – feeding can keep your cat healthy but according to most experts and vets, you should not consider "free – feeding" your cat because as previously mentioned, in the wild, these cats hunt and kill for food. It's not in their natural instinct that food is always available around them 24/7. That's not economic and it's also dangerous for their health. Cats are built to only eat small meals at a certain time (at least 5 – 6 hours ideally).

Generally cats are not grazers, and they can't just eat whenever. In the wild, they only eat food after doing an activity or after hunting for their prey, so if food is available to them anytime, it kinda messes with their brain and nature. Little did some owners know that free – feeding can lead to behavioral problems such as whenever they're peeing or pooping, if you want to train them to pee or poop at their litter box, you can at least have a chance to know when they're going to do it if you control their eating schedule. Of course, if you practice free – feeding you can expect them to relieve themselves anytime and anywhere they want which is not sanitary. It's highly recommended that you feed them small meal throughout the day instead of free – feeding your pet.

Types of Commercial Cat Foods

There are three major types of commercial cat foods; these are dry, semi moist, and canned. Dry food contains 6 to 10% moisture, semi moist is 15 to 30% and canned is 75%.

Most canned food has relatively more fat, protein and animal products and lesser carbohydrates than dry and semi-moist food. Pet food labels must list the percentage of protein, fat, fibre, and water in the food. Ask your veterinarian on how to properly read pet food labels so that you can get the most out of the food.

For adult Abyssinian cats, it is recommended that you give them dry foods because has two major benefits; the first one is that since it is dry, it won't eat a lot of food which of course would prevent overeating that could lead to obesity; and the second is that it will keep its teeth stronger because of chewing. If your cat prefers a much tastier wet food; you can mix a little bit of wet food in its dry meal to make it tastier.

Recommended Brands of Abyssinian Cat Foods

Feeding your cat a specific diet can make your pet's physique stay stronger, and its muscles will also stay supple. Another great benefit is that maintaining a healthy diet by combining protein rich foods (wet and dry) with vitamins can keep up your cat's appetite and also make them immune from diseases as they get older. Below are 5 of the most recommended cat food brands for your Abyssinian pet.

Goodlife Dry Cat Indoor Recipe

Goodlife is packed with a well – balanced amount of vitamins and minerals that your cat needs to stay healthy. It has a combination of meat topped with some vegetables to entice your cat even more. This branded cat food doesn't contain any wheat, soy or corns which are what is commonly used as fillers in other cat foods. Instead, it contains antioxidants that will help boost your cat's immune system. It also has crunchy morsels that can benefit your cat's teeth, and also provides as a practice for her paws.

It only costs about $25 for a 16 pound bag, and it is highly recommended among Abyssinian cat owners.

Purina Pro Plan Focus Canned Food

Another great food for your cat is Purina's Pro Plan Focus. It contains many essentials like a healthy metabolism formula. It is suited for weight management and kitten indoor care as well.

If you are looking to improve your cat's urinary tract, this is the best food to give to your Abyssinian cat because it has an Adult Urinary Tract Health Formula which reduces the pH levels in the urinary tract of your Abyssinian cat, in order to prevent Urinary Tract Infections (UTI) and other bladder infections.

It also contains about 12% protein that meet your cat's other dietary needs. You can also choose from different flavors like beef & chicken, ocean fish, and chicken. It cost around $20 for 24 pieces of 3 ounce cans and it can also serve as a great supplement for a dry food.

Merrick Before Grain

If you want a full – protein diet, Merrik's B.G. or Before Grain is one of the best cat foods you can also buy. It has two flavors – chicken, and salmon. It contains a lot of meat as well as essential vitamins and minerals.

Compared to other dry foods, it is quite expensive because it costs about $25 per bag (11 pounds), it is because this dry food contains more protein than vegetable fillers. According to most experts, if you buy protein filled cat foods, you are actually buying a premium quality because it doesn't contain fillers found in most standard cat foods. It focuses on what your cat actually needs – and that is protein.

Friskies Wet Cat Food

Friskies has been one of the most popular cat foods for several years now because they don't only provide good nutrition for cats, they also make it look more appealing through its variety of flavors. It's also one of the cheapest food brands out there. For only $15, you can already get 2 dozens of 5.5 ounce canned food.

It is available in Salmon & Beef, Chicken & Tuna, Ocean Whitefish & Tuna and also includes prime filets that cat's love. No wonder why this food brand is the best. You can use this wet food with a fortified dry food fof your cat.

Toxic Foods to Avoid

Some foods are toxic for cats in general. Make sure that your Abyssinian cat never gets to eat one of the toxic items below, and also ensure that the veterinary checks your cat every now and then. These harmful foods is as important as selecting the right supplements and food items for your cat. The following list of foods is highly toxic for your Abyssinian cats:

- Alcohol
- Apple seeds
- Avocado
- Cherry pits
- Chocolates
- Coffee
- Garlic
- Grapes/raisins
- Hops
- Ice Cream
- Macadamia nuts
- Mold
- Mushrooms
- Mustard seeds
- Onions/leeks
- Peach pits
- Potato leaves/stems
- Rhubarb leaves
- Tea
- Tomato leaves/stems
- Walnuts
- Xylitol
- Yeast dough

Tips in Feeding Your Abyssinian Cats

Whether you have a choosy or obsessive eater, your cat's needs to be fed properly, below are some tips on how to properly feed your cat so that feeding time can be more effective and enjoyable.

- Follow the Feeding Instructions and Recommended Daily Feeding Amounts on the packaging of your pet food. You can also consult your veterinarian regarding the feeding measurement.

- Place the recommended measured amount of food inside the bowl or dish each morning so your cat can eat as he or she pleases throughout the day.

- Monitor your cat's weight and adjust intake accordingly. The amount of food required to maintain an ideal body condition will vary depending on age, activity and environment.

- Reduce the daily intake of dry food to prevent overfeeding. Only if you feed your cat a combination of dry and wet food.

- Use a shallow bowl that your cat can grab food from without impeding the whiskers.

- Try placing the dish in the open to maximize sight lines. It also helps lessen the tension.

- Do not place your cat's dish in the corner of a room or on an edge because it's difficult to see the surroundings. This is also recommended with multiple cats.

- You can find also buy food accessories at your local pet store or even online. Its cost vary depending on the brand of the product

- Always check the feeders after use to make sure your cat is actually eating the recommended daily amount of food.

- For energetic cats, try dividing the daily portion into several bowls and place them in different locations throughout your home. This also helps to encourage your cat to discover sources of food throughout the day.

- Monitor the water intake to make sure your cat is properly hydrated. Use warm water for your kittens.

Feeding Amount and Frequency

Your Abyssinian's dietary requirements depends on many factors, for example, is your cat a house cat or a sort of yard cat or maybe both? Has he/she had sterilization surgery (spay/neuter)? It's vital to answer these questions because it will help answer you Abyssinian's dietary requirements. Their age, energy levels, previous conditions, size, weight etc. should be considered as to the amount needed to feed your cat. It's highly recommended that you consult your vet about it because they can identify what your pet needs in terms of its daily diet, the proper food ratio and the frequency. Once you learned about it, you should follow your vet's advice and stick to this kind of diet.

If you're Abyssinian gets obese, it is quite hard for them to lose weight, if this is the case, then you should immediately consult your vet to change the diet/meal plan for your cat to prevent further disorders such as diabetes.

In general though, you can refer to this table so you can have an idea on how much to feed your cat. Please be advice that it's highly recommended to consult your vet to know specific details about your cat's dietary needs.

Kittens

Weight	Age	Suggested Daily Intake
0.8 – 1.3 pounds	1 – 2 months	25 – 35 grams
1.4 – 2.6 pounds	2 – 3 months	40 – 50 grams
2. 7 – 4.0 pounds	3 – 4 months	50 – 55 grams

Adult Cats

Weight	Suggested Daily Intake Per Body - Type		
	Lean	Normal	Overweight
4 pounds	30 grams	30 grams	20 grams
6 pounds	45 grams	45 grams	30 grams
8 pounds	70 grams	60 grams	45 grams
10 pounds	90 grams	70 grams	45 grams
12 pounds	--	90 grams	60 grams
14 pounds	--		70 grams

Chapter Six: Grooming and Training Your Abyssinian Cats

After knowing how to feed your gorgeous Abyssinians a proper diet and nutrition, it's now time to learn how to groom them, and also train them. Abyssinian cats are one of the most intelligent feline breeds; they are naturally curious and can usually understand how things work around the house especially if you start training them at a young age. In terms of grooming, you won't have a problem with them because they don't shed a lot compared to other furry cats.

In this chapter you'll learn some tips on how to train them, keep them clean and appealing as well as learn how to handle their sometimes naughty behavior.

Guidelines in Training Your Abyssinian Cats

Training your cat is both a rewarding and beneficial experience for your pet and for you as its owner. You'll get a chance to bond with them, and also learn what makes them tick. There are lots of pet owners out there who have properly trained and raised a well-behaved Abyssinians. As previously mentioned, these cats are clever creatures, and curious by nature which is good because they'll be able to absorb information very quickly and easily.

Trust is the most important key in training your cat. The first thing you need to do is to be able to establish a solid connection and rapport between you and your pet.

Here are some general guidelines on how to train your cat:

- Decide on the suitable hand signal. Whistling and hand clapping are ideal because you can give the signal at any time.

- Avoid using bells or other signaling devices, because it may not be effective during emergencies.

- Train your cat when it is hungry. You can offer some treats if it follows a command from you. For best results, keep repeating this exercise until the cat/kitten gets used to it.

- Teach your cats different commands such as positions and litter box training.

- Use food treats or positive reinforcement once it follows and repeat the exercises over and over again.

- When it comes to litter training, you should take your kitten to the litter box and place him inside. He may scratch around a little bit or he might jump right out. He/she will get used to it; you're doing this because you want them to be familiar with the purpose of the litter box/pan.

- Just keep putting your kitten in the litter box a few times a day for the first few days until he gets used to the location. You should also make sure that it is in a quiet, easy to reach location.

- If you have more than one Abyssinian cat, you should also have more than one litter box. The best rule of thumb to follow is one litter box per cat plus one extra.

- Set up your litter boxes in a quiet, private place that is easy to access. If you have a dog or other pets in the house you may need to place the box somewhere he can't get to it.

- Make sure that the litter box you choose is large enough for your cat to get into and move around easily. There are many different types of litter boxes to choose from so you have plenty of options.

- Don't let too much litter add up on the box, otherwise it'll be unsanitary. Scoop it frequently and clean it thoroughly. This can also prevent your cat from eating their own poo.

- Don't also add too much fragrance inside the litter box after you clean it as these things could aggravate allergies to your Abyssinian cat.

Guidelines in Grooming Your Abyssinian Cats

Your cat's skin produces natural oils that help to protect his skin and keep it moisturized. Grooming for cats is not just about keeping it clean, it is mainly about improving and maintaining the condition of the skin. Grooming your cat helps to distribute its natural body oils to keep his skin healthy, silky, and soft. Here are some general guidelines on how to bathe/groom your cat:

- You should bath your cat about once or twice a week or at least every other day. If you do it regularly, your cat will get used to it and it will not become a major chore.
- Fill your tub or a large sink with about 1 – 2 inches of lukewarm water. This is already enough to get your cat's skin damp. Don't fill the tub up to the brim or more than what is required. They could drown or might get sick.
- Use a baby shampoo or something that is very mild, and fragrance-free. Massage it into your cat's skin by hand or using a soft cloth.
- After bathing, use a soft cloth and some warm water to remove all traces of soap. Once your cat gets used to the bathing process it may tolerate you pouring water over his back to rinse it.

How to Brush Your Cat's Teeth

Periodontal disease can cause health issues in cats which is why it is important in keeping your cat's teeth clean. Many cat owners neglect their cat's dental health which is a serious mistake. Brushing your cat's teeth is fairly easy, though you will need a special pet tooth brush and pet toothpaste to do it.

You may also need to get your cat accustomed to the toothbrush and the tooth-brushing process. Ideally you should be brushing your cat's teeth every day but if he will only let you do it a few times a week then that is certainly better than nothing.

How to Trim Your Cat's Nails

Your cat's nails grow in the same way that your own nails grow so they need to be trimmed occasionally. Most pet owners find that trimming their cat's nails once a week or twice a month is sufficient. Before you trim your cat's nails for the first time you should have your veterinarian or a professional groomer show you how to do it.

Cleaning Your Cat's Ears

Abyssinian cats have quite a large, alert looking, and open ears, which is why you do not have to worry as much about ear infections as you might with other breeds. Ear infections are most common in breeds that have folded ears because it limits the amount of air flow to the inner portion of the ear because wet ears are a breeding ground for bacteria. It is still ideal to clean your cat's ears occasionally just to remove normal wax buildup.

To clean its ears, use a cat ear cleaning solution and squeeze a few drops into the ear canal. Massage the base of your cat's ears to distribute the solution, and then wipe it away using a clean cotton balls.

Tips on How to Deal with Your Cat's Behavior

Scratching Behavior

When it comes to things like scratching, you should not try to completely eradicate this behavior, this is because scratching is a normal and important behavior for cats because it helps them to stretch their toes and to spread their scent through glands in the pads of their feet.

If your cat is scratching up your furniture, the solution may be as simple as providing him with scratching posts around the house. To encourage your cat to use them instead of your furniture, sprinkle them with dried catnip or use a liquid catnip spray. When your cat uses the scratching post, give him a couple of treats as well to encourage him.

Loud Behavior or Attention – Seeking Cats

Sometimes cats can develop a tendency toward demanding attention because they don't do well in isolation.

As mentioned earlier, they are an affectionate breed, and they don't like being left alone. It is important to understand that this is the nature of the Abyssinian breed, and most cats for that matter. You can, however, reduce annoying behaviors like incessant 'meowing' by not giving in to your cat.

If he 'meows' at you for attention and you give it to him you will only be reinforcing that behavior. If you want your cat to leave you alone while you are working on the computer, for example, just ignore him until he gives up. Eventually your cat will learn when it is play time and when it is not.

Chapter Seven: Showing Your Abyssinian Cats

Abyssinian cats are eligible for showing. So if you are interested in letting your gorgeous and sturdy cat show off its beauty and true magnificence, why not sign up for several cat competitions? It can vary from training competitions to sort of like a cat – walk type of events. It's no wonder that your cat has the potential to be so much more than just a house cat, but before you show your pet, you have to make sure that he/she meets the requirements for the breed standard and also learn some basic tips on how to prepare yourself and your pet so you can take home the gold!

In this chapter you will learn more about the specific standard for the Abyssinian breed, and also some guidelines on how to prepare your pet for a show. This information will help you to decide if showing your Abyssinian cat is really something you want to do.

Cat Fanciers' Association Abyssinian Breed Standard

Scoring System

Total Points (100)

Head – 25 points

- Muzzle – 6 points
- Skull – 6 points
- Ears – 7 points
- Eye Shape – 6 points

Body – 30 points

- Torso – 15 points
- Legs and Feet – 10 points
- Tail – 5 points

Coat – 10 points

- Texture – 10 points

Color – 35 points

- Color – 15 points
- Ticking – 15 points
- Eye Color – 5 points

General

- Must be a colorful cat with a ticked coat
- Must be medium – size and should show a hard and muscular body structure
- Must appear active, lively and enthusiastic
- Should be physically, and temperamentally well – balanced
- Must have pass the specific requirements of the breed standard.

Head

- Should have a rounded wedge, and modified head without flat planes
- The profile, and cheek as well as the eye brows should all show a gentle contour

- There should be a slight rise from the nose's bridge to its forehead

Muzzle

- Must not be too pointy or square
- The chin shouldn't be protruding or receding
- There should be an allowance in jowls for males

Ears

- Should be alert, quite pointed, and large
- Must also be broad and cupped at its base
- The hairs on the ears should be short and must be lying flat

Eyes

- Must be almond in shape
- Should be large, bright, and expressive
- Must not be round or oriental looking
- It should also be accentuated with a dark line encircled with a light colored area

Body

- Should be medium and relatively long
- Must have a well – developed muscular structure that appears graceful and should not have a coarseness
- Must be proportionate and well – balance

Legs and Feet

- Must be slim, fine boned, and proportionate
- Must appear to be on tip toe when standing
- The paws should be oval, small, and compact
- Should have complete toes (5 in front; 4 behind)

Tail

- Should be thick, relatively long, and tapering

Coat

- Must have a soft, fine, and silky coat
- It should also be dense, and lustrous
- Must also be medium in length

Coat Color

- Should be warm and glowing

Ticking

- Must be distinct and even, preferably with dark colored bands and must be in contrast with undercoat colored bands on its hair shafts.

- The undercoat must be clear and bright to the skin
- A deeper color shade is preferred

Eye Color

- Must be gold or green
- The richer color, the better

With Penalty

- Off – color pads
- A narrow head that is long or a short round head
- If he/she has barring on its legs
- Rings on tail
- Has a dark broken necklace markings
- White undercoat on blue or fawn – colored cats
- Grey tone in its coat

Disqualification

- If the cat has a white locket or has a white spot on any parts except the nostrils, chin, or upper throat area.
- If the cat has a kinked or has abnormal tail
- If there's a grey undercoat that is close to the skin and extends throughout the body.
- If there's a black hair on a red – colored cat.

Guidelines before Presenting Your Abyssinian Cat

Showing your cat can be a wonderful experience but it can also be quite challenging. In order to ensure that your cat does well in the show, he needs to be a strong example of the breed standard. Make sure that you familiarized yourself with the rules and regulations for a particular show in which you plan to enter your cat.

In addition to making sure that your cat meets the qualifications of the breed standard, there are also some general things you can do to prepare for a cat show. Here are some guidelines in preparing your cat for show:

- Make sure your cat is properly pedigreed according to the regulations of the show – you may need to present your cat's papers/ license as proof so make sure to have them ready.

- Make sure to fill out the registration form correctly, providing all of the necessary details, and turn it in on time
- Prepare to pay an entry fee as well or a competition fee if any.

- Clip your cat's claws before the show – declawed cats are allowed as well without penalty.

- Make sure that your cat is registered with the organization running the show.

- Make sure to enter your cat in the proper age bracket or category because some organizations allow kittens as young as 3 months while other have some restrictions.

- Find out what is provided by the show and what you need to bring for yourself – some competitions provide an exhibition cage but you will need to bring some things.

- Be prepared to spend all day at the show and bring with you everything you and your cat may need to make it through the day.

- Pay close attention to all of the information the show gives you with your registration, some shows provide a list of recommended materials to bring either through their website or it may be directly sent to your email.

Below are the lists of things you need to bring before the show:

- Your cat's pedigree and registration papers.
- Veterinary records and proof of vaccinations.
- Litter pan and cat litter (if not provided).

- Food treats, and food/water bowls.
- Cage curtains and clips to hang them.
- A blanket or bed for the cage.
- Any necessary grooming equipment, nail clippers.
- Confirmation slip received at entry.
- Food, water, and extra clothes for yourself.
- Garbage bag for clean-up.

Chapter Eight: Breeding Your Abyssinian Cats

If you have grown fond of your Abyssinian cat already, and you feel like you're ready to take care more of these adorable creatures, maybe it's now time for you to know how to breed them, and raise Abyssinian kittens on your own! Who knows? You could become a reputable breeder some day!

In this chapter you'll be provided with information about sexual dimorphism for Abyssinian cats, breeding basics, their mating process, and the things you need to prepare for your newborn kittens.

Sexual Dimorphism

Abyssinian cats are sexually dimorphic animals like most cats, and mammals in general. It means that their sex can be identified based from their physical characteristics or structure, and of course by looking at their reproductive organs. The differences in terms of its appearance in a male or a female cat is actually subtle; males are usually larger and heavier than female cats.

Breeding Basics

In general, cats have an estrous or heat cycle, (similar to most female creatures and even humans). The female cats also known as the queen usually enters her first heat or sexual maturity as young as three – four months. Females cats generally has two to three heat cycles during the breeding season that usually occurs around February to October. Female cats are also induced ovulators which mean that they do not ovulate unless they are bred with a male cat. This greatly increases the chances of conception when bred.

Signs that Your Female Cats is ready for Mating

There are many signs that the queen is undergoing its heat cycle. If you notice your Abyssinian cat doing the following that means that she is ready for mating, and she is looking for a mate. Male or tom cats naturally know if a female is ready for mating through these signs:

- Rolling (sign that they are flirting)
- Rubbing against objects
- She is kneading her back feet
- Usually makes repeated, long, and loud sounds to signal or call a tom cat
- Female cats usually spread a scent or smell during their heat cycle so that tom cats can smell it, and once they do they will be around that female cat until she is ready for mating.

These behaviors can last up to more than ten days and can repeat in more than three months if the queen is not bred. If the queen is bred, the cycle ends as her body prepares for pregnancy.

Mating Process

When you bred your female Abyssinian cat to a tom cat (either the same breed or a different cat breed), you can expect the mating to last for around ten minutes or more. Once the queen shrieks or screams loudly that means that their mating is done. However, as long as you cat is still on her heat cycle, she can still mate whenever she's ready or if not, she won't entertain or pay attention in any tom cat after the cycle was finished

Usually a Queen would keep on licking herself to prepare for the next mating session. The interval between mating sessions could be around a few minutes up to a few hours. It is also not necessary that a female cat would go back to the same tom cat next day which could result in producing kittens with multiple fathers. If you don't want any unwanted pregnancies you should keep her away from other male cats to prevent more mating or more kittens until she gives birth. If you notice your cat has an increase appetite, a swollen mammary gland, or is developing a large abdomen that means your cat is already pregnant.

Pregnancy FAQs

How long should I wait before my cat gives birth?

In the feline world, pregnancy is called gestation. Gestation period for Abyssinians usually lasts for about 65 to 67 days or around 6 weeks. Usually after 3 weeks of its pregnancy period, you'll notice that her nipples start to turn pinkish in color as a sign that milk is being produced by the body. After the 5th week or a few days before giving birth, your cat will be ready to lactate once she gives birth.

How do cats give birth?

Well like most mammals, mother cats will have contractions once they are ready to give birth. Usually these contractions decrease in two to three minutes. Once you see a water bubble of amniotic fluid, it indicates that a kitten is in the birth canal already and can come out any second. The birth interval of kittens is typically fifteen to thirty minutes. Once she is done giving birth, the mother cat will eat the placenta to unwrap its kitten from the amniotic sac membranes that cover its newborn's muzzle. The mother cat should break these by licking to enable the kitten to breath. The mother cat will also chew through the cord and eat the placenta, which is normal and nutritionally valuable for her. Don't be surprise if your female cat does this.

Can I help my cat during labor?

Yes of course! They don't need it but it won't hurt! However, before you do make sure that you consult your veterinarian first or study and/or ask breeders on how to do aid your cat properly. You can also help by preparing things such as a clean cloth, nesting box, gloves, scissors, bedding, or other kitten essentials

How many kittens should I expect?

Abyssinian cats typically give birth to 6 kittens on average and up to a maximum of 12 kittens. These kittens also tend to grow at an average rate and reach maturity after about 24 weeks.

When do kittens become mature or independent?

Kittens become mature around 6 months of age. They'll begin to leave their moms. Once they become a year old, you can expect them to be matured and developed to a full adult size and weight.

How is it possible to have multiple fathers?

Queens can be bred by more than one male during a heat period, the semen of male cats can stay inside the queen for a period of time even if the queen or female cat have already mated with other male cats, resulting in kittens from the same litter with different fathers.

What is Pseudo – pregnancy?

Pseudo-pregnancy is the term for false pregnancy in cats. This typically begins at the end of estrus, and can last for several months. Consult your veterinarian to determine if your cat is pregnant for real or not.

Raising Kittens

After giving birth, the Queen will want to spend time with her kittens in a typically quiet or secluded spot; she will also feed them through her mammary glands. Make sure to provide your cat with a comfortable bed, and feed it properly with the right nutrition as well. It is highly advisable that you consult your vet on the proper amount and/or ideal diet for your female cat before and after giving birth so that she can regain her strength as quickly as possible.

It's also ideal that you bring your newborn kittens to the vet to make sure that they are healthy, and for you to also know what to do in making them strong against diseases since they are still at a vulnerable stage. It could be ideal to know the vaccinations they'll need as they grow older so that you can also prepare financially. Your vet can also advise you on the proper diet for these new kittens or as soon as they reached a few weeks of maturity.

Provide your newborn kittens a comfy bedding and make sure to place it near their mothers as they will still need to feed from their mom's milk.

Don't groom or bath them yet because they are not yet mature for that, their mother's will take care of the grooming part by licking them. You also would want to protect them from your other household pets if any because they may mistake the kittens as a food.

The most fun part is that once they grow a little bit older, you can now feed them kibbles or a recommended kitten diet, you can also play with them, and train them at an early age. You should also make sure that the house temperature is at a normal range.

Chapter Nine: Common Diseases and Health Requirements

In this chapter you will be provided with some of the most common health problems affecting Abyssinian cats. If you are aware of the possible diseases and disorders that may cause trouble for your pet, it can be potentially lifesaving and also economic! As what they always say, prevention is better than cure. You as the potential cat keeper should also learn how to strengthen your cat's resistance to common illnesses by giving them the necessary vaccinations and through having regular checkup with their vets. Remember that a healthy cat is a happy cat!

Common Health Problems

In this section, you will learn about the diseases that may affect and threaten your Abyssinian cat. Learning these diseases as well as its remedies is vital for you and your cat so that you could prevent it from happening or even help with its treatment in case they caught one.

Minor Problems:

Dental Disease

There's nothing more damaging to the heart, liver, and kidney of cats than infected teeth. According to surveys, cats that are above 3 years old have dental disease or otherwise known as periodontal disease. It is a type of cavity that vets called tooth desorption.

The most common sign is a red and tire gums or mostly broken and damaged teeth. Unfortunately, most owners fail to check their cat's dental health; often time's owners notice signs at a very late stage which results to a lot of work to be done and/or causes major troubles in a cat's health.

Atopy

Cats, like humans can suffer from an itchy skin. This form of allergy in cats is known as "atopy." The affected areas are the legs, belly, face, and ears. Signs of atopy are licking or over grooming the affected areas, rubbing its face and regular ear infections. Sometimes, you may notice thinner or shortened hair as well as sore skin lesions. Such signs usually appear between 1 to 3 years old and can get worse every year. Mites may also be the cause of the problem since they have similar signs. The great thing is that there are many treatment options available for this condition. Consult your veterinarian to know the best treatment for your cat's atopy.

Arthritis

Cats are also prone to arthritis. In fact, about 90% of cats have arthritis. It is a chronic and painful disease that fortunately is highly treatable. What most owners don't know is that cats are good in hiding symptoms of pain because it is their natural inclination in the wild; this is why routine vet checkup is highly recommended to give your pet a thorough examination.

Major Problems:

Kidney Diseases

Kidney disease is next on the list of silent, common but treatable diseases. If you diagnose a cat with early stage kidney disease, you can lengthen its life for many years. Just switching to a diet made for kidney disease buys your pet more time to not further damage their kidneys and enable the body to repair itself. The most important thing though is to catch it early because usually owners don't notice any sign of renal failure at all, and by the time such symptoms are obvious, 75% of the kidney's function has already been loss.

It's highly advisable that every time you go to your vet, make sure that your cat will undergo complete routine check including a blood sample or other laboratory processes. One example is by using urine or blood screening for diagnosis. Elderly cats are prone to kidney disease, so the only prevention is for your pet to start treatment early on before it progresses to a more serious condition.

Hypertension

Most owners don't know how to measure their cat's blood pressure as well as listen to its heart beat for any sign of heart diseases. High blood pressure is common in older cats as well, and those who already have kidney and thyroid illnesses are much prone in developing hypertension which can damage your cat's health in a massive way.

Heart Disease

Another most common illness among cats species is heart disease, but with proper medication, well – balanced diet, and regular check-up can prevent further illnesses such as strokes or other complications. Two of the most fatal and common heart diseases among cats are the following:

- Feline Aortic Thromboembolism (FATE)
- Congestive Heart Failure

o **Feline Aortic Thromboembolism (FATE)** - this disease is also known as Arterial Thromboembolism. If your cats have this disease it will eventually develop blood clots in their arteries usually found a part of the aorta which is the large blood vessel that supplies blood from the heart to the body. It blocks the normal blood flow to the hind legs that causes paralysis of both hind legs, and sometimes even become cold or painful. The main sign that your cat is suffering from FATE is its sudden inability to walk or if the cat is dragging one or both hind legs and crying. Once you notice this, seek medical care as soon as possible, your pet needs emergency care because it is fatal. Arterial Thromboembolisms is a life-threatening disease, so as soon as you learned that your cat is suffering from this disease, consult a veterinarian immediately because this requires quick action and prolonged medical care. Cats who survive thromboembolisms, however, usually regain full function of their limbs. If your cat is diagnosed with heart disease, veterinarians may prescribe medications to help lower the risk of blood clots.

○ **Congestive Heart Failure -** In the early stages of congestive heart failure, most cats don't show any signs at all, with this disease cats starts to build up fluids in the chest, and most cats are able to hide any signs until it is fairly advance. Most owners as usual, do not notice any signs because the cat seems perfectly normal, then all of a sudden they became gravely ill like it just happened overnight but the truth is, the disease has been progressing for months and sometimes years! If you take your cat to the vet regularly, doctors can quickly identify abnormal heart rate or rhythm of your pet which is of course beneficial so that your cat can be treated efficiently.

Hyperthyroidism

This disease is commonly because of a hyper tumor development. Tumors can be benign and not cancerous, however it can cause the thyroids to produce excess hormones which messes up the cat's metabolism and cause things like weight loss, nausea, behavioral changes as well as heart and kidney problems. Like any other diseases, hyperthyroidism can be treated through proper diet and medication but if it is left untreated, it can cause fatality.

Diabetes

Diabetes Mellitus is a genetic and hereditary disease that can occur in any cat breed. Cats can be diabetic regardless of other health problems.

Other cats may have a susceptibility to diabetes, but will only become overtly diabetic if they are allowed to become overweight or eat a poor diet. If a cat's weight and diet are managed appropriately, the risk for diabetes in your pet is much lower. The main cause of diabetes in cats is inactive lifestyles.

If your cat just likes to eat a lot and be lazy all the time, it may be the root cause of this disease that is why exercise is very important to prevent diabetes. Major symptom of diabetes includes weight loss despite of a good appetite, excessive thirst, and increased urination. It is also ideal to undergo some tests for at least once a year and more often as your cat ages, because older cats are much prone to becoming diabetic.

The worst case scenario is that your cat may need insulin injections to treat its diabetes, but usually many diabetic cats do not need to receive insulin injections if they lose weight, they just need to switch to a high-protein, low-carbohydrate prescription diet.

Diabetes are thought to be hereditary, that is why managing the type and quantity of food that your pet eats and incorporating exercise into your cat's daily routine is very vital! Daily exercise and proper diet is important in keeping your cat active and energetic. If your cat is slim or fit, it can highly prevent illnesses related to weight gain.

Diabetes can also be related to a painful condition called pancreatitis. Chronic pancreatitis, which is thought to be genetically inherited, can lead to damage of the cells in the pancreas that produce insulin, and therefore can lead to a diabetic state in the cat. Always consult your veterinarian if you feel like your cat is suffering from diabetes.

Feline Lower Urinary Tract Disease (FLUTD)

This disease is the inability to control the bladder muscles, which is usually due to improper nerve function from a spinal defect. Urinary defect is rare in cats so if you notice that your cat is urinating in improper locations, it may be suffering from FLUTD and is trying to get you to notice.

Watch out for any signs of abnormal urination such as urinating on a tile floor, bathtub or any other cool surface. Some early symptoms also include a blood in the urine; small amount or no urine at all as well as unusual crying in the litter box. Cats that are previously diagnosed with urinary tract infection, bladder stones are also prone to Feline Lower Urinary Tract Disease. If your cat demonstrates any of these symptoms, bring it to a veterinarian right away, because this can become an emergency within only a few hours. The inability to urinate is painful and quickly fatal, especially for male cats, if its urethra is blocked with stones or crystals, the urine will be blocked.

An important reminder to prevent such disease is to always bring your cat to a clinic for a regular urinalysis testing. This test allows us to check for signs of infection, kidney disease, crystals in the urine, and even diabetes. You can also perform other tests such as X-rays and ultrasounds because it can also help detect the presence of stones in the bladder or kidneys.

If you brought your pet early to the vet, lower urinary tract disease can be controlled with medications and special diets, though in some severe cases of FLUTD it may also require surgery.

Kidney Failure

Renal failure is another fatal disease that can evolve from previous urinary tract problems, this is the inability of the kidneys to properly drain toxins and cleanse the waste in the blood. If your cat has renal failure it will not properly perform its function of regulating hydration. Kidney disease is extremely common in older cats. This disease is often due to exposure to toxins or genetic causes in young cats. It is hereditary and passed on from one generation to another. Even very young kittens can have renal failure if they have inherited kidney defects from their mothers and fathers.

The best preventive measure is to perform screening tests for kidney problems as early as 2 months old, make sure to also regularly screen your pet throughout its entire lifetime because sometimes, it doesn't show up in the first few test. Severe renal failure is a progressive, fatal disease, sometimes called a "slow death" but special diets and medications can help cats with kidney diseases live longer, fuller lives if treated early.

Recommended Vaccinations

Cats are generally healthy but they can still catch different bacterial and viral infections from time to time. Fortunately, it can be prevented through vaccination. Core Vaccines are highly recommended if the risk of your cat contracting these diseases is high.

In addition, vaccines are available to offer protection from other potential dangerous diseases like feline leukemia and other fatal virus.

The vaccination recommendations listed below for your cat highly depends on the availability in your area, your cat's age, and any other risk factors specific to its lifestyle, consult your vet for further information:

- Panleukopenia
- Rhinotracheitis
- Calicivirus
- Rabies
- Feline Leukemia
- Chlamydophila
- Feline Infectious Peritonitis
- Bordetella
- Giardia
- Feline Immunodeficiency Virus

Vaccination Schedule for Cats and Kittens

For kittens aged 6 - 7 weeks old, combination of vaccines, which is consists of feline distemper, rhinotracheitis, and calicivirus is needed. For kittens that are 10 weeks old, combination of vaccines is needed plus Chlamydophila or Pneumonitis for during this age, they are prone to respiratory diseases.

For kittens that are 12 - 13 weeks old and up (age may vary according to local law), generally they need to have a rabies vaccine as well as feline leukemia vaccine (FeLV), because at this age kittens can be exposed to feline leukemia virus, these vaccines can be given by your local veterinarian.

For adult cats, aside from combination of vaccines booster, cats also need Chlamydophila or Pneumonitis vaccine, feline leukemia vaccine (FeLV), as well as rabies vaccine.

Consult with your local veterinarian to determine the appropriate vaccination schedule for your cat. Remember, recommendations vary depending on the age, breed, and health status of the cat, the potential of the cat to be exposed to the disease, the type of vaccine, whether the cat is used for breeding, and the geographical area where the cat lives or may visit.

Chapter Ten: Care Sheet and Summary

Now that you have basic knowledge on how to take care of an Abyssinian breed, it's time for you to apply it, and of course get to learn new things! You can search online for more info about the breed or some additional info on how to make them healthy and happy, and how you can become a great keeper and a potentially reputable breeder.

In this chapter, we will give you the quick summary of the major points you need to remember that was discussed in this book. A quick glance can be of help if you are in a hurry or if you simply wanted to review something important. Thank you for reading! Never stop learning though!

Biological Information

Taxonomy: Kingdom Animalia, Phylum Chordata, Class Mammalia, Order Carnivora, Family Felidae, Genus Felis Species Domesticus.

Country of Origin: Ethiopia, Egypt

Breed Size: medium – size breed

Body Type and Appearance: Has a muscular yet slender type body with long legs, sharp eyes, large ears, short tail and broad head.

Weight: average of 8 – 12 pounds

Coat Length: short ticked coat

Coat Texture: fine, silky, smooth, soft

Color: lavender or lilac, chocolate, black, silver, blue, fawn (pale tan), cinnamon, ruddy (bluish – gray), and dark brown

Other Names: Ticked Cat, British Tick Cat, Bunny Cat, Rabbit Cat, Hare Cat, Aby Cat

Abyssinian Cats as Pets

Temperament: Intelligent, witty, fun, and affectionate breed, active, quite docile, also perfect for children particularly those who are around 6 – 8 years old.

Other pets: These cats are also quite fearless to other animals friendly with other household pets such as dogs, other cat breeds, rabbits, guinea pigs and the like

Major Pro: Smart, loyal, obedient, curious, active, and fun cats; can be easily trained, and very affectionate

Major Con: Not the usual lap cat

Legal Requirements and Cat Licensing:

United States: There are no federal requirements for licensing either cats or even dogs. It is regulated at the state level.

United Kingdom: You will need to get a special permit if you plan to travel with your cat into or out of the country. Pets are also subject to quarantine.

Other countries: Bring proper documents such as your state permit for your cat, rabies or vaccinations certificate, and current health condition. Other requirements as deemed necessary.

Purchasing and Selecting a Healthy Breed

Where to Purchase: Backyard/Private Breeders, Online Stores, Cat Conventions or Pet Conferences

Characteristics of a Reputable Breeder: Expect a reputable breeder to ask you questions about yourself as well. A responsible breeder wants to make sure that his cats go to good homes.

Characteristics of a Healthy Breed: Examine the cat's or kitten's body thoroughly for any signs of illness and potential injuries. The kitten/s should be active, and playful, interacting with each other in a healthy way.

Habitat Requirements for Abyssinian Cats: The bigger the bed, the better for your pet! Provide play pen, perches, toys and other essential accessories.

Housing Temperature: should still be at a normal range, not too hot and not too cold.

Nutrition and Food

- Abyssinian cats must be given eat protein – rich foods as well as some healthy fats as part of their diet.

Recommended Brands of Abyssinian Cat Foods: Goodlife Dry Cat Indoor Recipe, Purina Pro Plan, Focus Canned Food, Merrick Before Grain, Friskies Wet Cat Food

How to Feed Your Cat: Follow the Feeding Instructions and Recommended Daily Feeding Amounts on the packaging of your pet food. You can also consult your veterinarian regarding the feeding measurement.

Feeding Amount/Frequency: Their age, energy levels, previous conditions, size, weight etc. should be considered as to the amount needed to feed your cat. It's highly recommended that you consult your vet about it because they can identify what your pet needs in terms of its daily diet, the proper food ratio and the frequency. (See table in Chapter 5 for reference)

Grooming and Training Your Abyssinian Cats

How to Brush Your Cat's Teeth: Ideally you should be brushing your cat's teeth every day

How to Trim Your Cat's Nails: Once a week or twice a month is sufficient

Cleaning Your Cat's Ears: It is still ideal to clean your cat's ears occasionally just to remove normal wax buildup_use a cat ear cleaning solution and squeeze a few drops into the ear canal

Showing Your Abyssinian Cats:

- Must be a colorful cat with a ticked coat

- Must be medium – size and should show a hard and muscular body structure

- Must appear active, lively and enthusiastic

- Should be physically, and temperamentally well – balanced

- Must have pass the specific requirements of the breed standard.

(See Breed Standard in Chapter 7 for complete list)

Breeding Your Abyssinian Cats

Gestation Period: 65 to 67 days or around 6 weeks

Litter Size: Abyssinian cats typically give birth to 6 kittens on average and up to a maximum of 12 kittens

Maturity: Kittens become mature around 6 months of age

Common Diseases and Health Requirements

- **Minor Diseases:**
- Dental Disease
- Atopy
- Arthritis
- **Major Diseases:**
- Kidney Diseases
- Hypertension
- Heart Diseases
  - Feline Aortic Thromboembolism (FATE)
  - Congestive Heart Failure
- Hyperthyroidism
- Diabetes
- Feline Lower Urinary Tract Disease (FLUTD)
- Kidney Failure

Recommended Vaccinations:

- Panleukopenia
- Rhinotracheitis
- Calicivirus
- Rabies
- Feline Leukemia
- Chlamydophila
- Feline Infectious Peritonitis
- Bordetella

- Giardia
- Feline Immunodeficiency Virus

Glossary of Cat Terms

Abundism – Referring to a cat that has markings more prolific than is normal.

Acariasis – A type of mite infection.

ACF – Australian Cat Federation

Affix – A cattery name that follows the cat's registered name; cattery owner, not the breeder of the cat.

Agouti – A type of natural coloring pattern in which individual hairs have bands of light and dark coloring.

Ailurophile – A person who loves cats.

Albino – A type of genetic mutation which results in little to no pigmentation, in the eyes, skin, and coat.

Allbreed – Referring to a show that accepts all breeds or a judge who is qualified to judge all breeds.

Alley Cat – A non-pedigreed cat.

Alter – A desexed cat; a male cat that has been neutered or a female that has been spayed.

Amino Acid – The building blocks of protein; there are 22 types for cats, 11 of which can be synthesized and 11 which must come from the diet (see essential amino acid).

Anestrus – The period between estrus cycles in a female cat.

Any Other Variety (AOV) – A registered cat that doesn't conform to the breed standard.

ASH – American Shorthair, a breed of cat.

Back Cross – A type of breeding in which the offspring is mated back to the parent.

Balance – Referring to the cat's structure; proportional in accordance with the breed standard.

Barring – Describing the tabby's striped markings.

Base Color – The color of the coat.

Bicolor – A cat with patched color and white.

Blaze – A white coloring on the face, usually in the shape of an inverted V.

Bloodline – The pedigree of the cat.

Brindle – A type of coloring, a brownish or tawny coat with streaks of another color.

Castration – The surgical removal of a male cat's testicles.

Cat Show – An event where cats are shown and judged.

Cattery – A registered cat breeder; also, a place where cats may be boarded.

CFA – The Cat Fanciers Association.

Cobby – A compact body type.

Colony – A group of cats living wild outside.

Color Point – A type of coat pattern that is controlled by color point alleles; pigmentation on the tail, legs, face, and ears with an ivory or white coat.

Colostrum – The first milk produced by a lactating female; contains vital nutrients and antibodies.

Conformation – The degree to which a pedigreed cat adheres to the breed standard.

Cross Breed – The offspring produced by mating two distinct breeds.

Dam – The female parent.

Declawing – The surgical removal of the cat's claw and first toe joint.

Developed Breed – A breed that was developed through selective breeding and crossing with established breeds.

Down Hairs – The short, fine hairs closest to the body which keep the cat warm.

DSH – Domestic Shorthair.

Estrus – The reproductive cycle in female cats during which she becomes fertile and receptive to mating.

Fading Kitten Syndrome – Kittens that die within the first two weeks after birth; the cause is generally unknown.

Feral – A wild, untamed cat of domestic descent.

Gestation – Pregnancy; the period during which the fetuses develop in the female's uterus.

Guard Hairs – Coarse, outer hairs on the coat.

Harlequin – A type of coloring in which there are van markings of any color with the addition of small patches of the same color on the legs and body.

Inbreeding – The breeding of related cats within a closed group or breed.

Kibble – Another name for dry cat food.

Lilac – A type of coat color that is pale pinkish-gray.

Line – The pedigree of ancestors; family tree.

Litter – The name given to a group of kittens born at the same time from a single female.

Mask – A type of coloring seen on the face in some breeds.

Matts – Knots or tangles in the cat's fur.

Mittens – White markings on the feet of a cat.

Moggie – Another name for a mixed breed cat.

Mutation – A change in the DNA of a cell.

Muzzle – The nose and jaws of an animal.

Natural Breed – A breed that developed without selective breeding or the assistance of humans.

Neutering – Desexing a male cat.

Open Show – A show in which spectators are allowed to view the judging.

Pads – The thick skin on the bottom of the feet.

Particolor – A type of coloration in which there are markings of two or more distinct colors.

Patched – A type of coloration in which there is any solid color, tabby, or tortoiseshell color plus white.

Pedigree – A purebred cat; the cat's papers showing its family history.

Pet Quality – A cat that is not deemed of high enough standard to be shown or bred.

Piebald – A cat with white patches of fur.

Points – Also color points; markings of contrasting color on the face, ears, legs, and tail.

Pricked – Referring to ears that sit upright.

Purebred – A pedigreed cat.

Queen – An intact female cat.

Roman Nose – A type of nose shape with a bump or arch.

Scruff – The loose skin on the back of a cat's neck.

Selective Breeding – A method of modifying or improving a breed by choosing cats with desirable traits.

Senior – A cat that is more than 5 but less than 7 years old.

Sire – The male parent of a cat.

Solid – Also self; a cat with a single coat color.

Spay – Desexing a female cat.

Stud – An intact male cat.

Tabby – A type of coat pattern consisting of a contrasting color over a ground color.

Tom Cat – An intact male cat.

Tortoiseshell – A type of coat pattern consisting of a mosaic of red or cream and another base color.

Tri-Color – A type of coat pattern consisting of three distinct colors in the coat.

Tuxedo – A black and white cat.

Unaltered – A cat that has not been desexed.

Index

C

D

E

F

G

L

M

N

Photo Credits

Page 1 Photo by user auenleben via Pixabay.com, https://pixabay.com/en/cat-kitten-abyssinian-cat-s-eyes-2204333/

Page 4 Photo by user skeeze via Pixabay.com, https://pixabay.com/en/abyssinian-cat-feline-egyptian-zula-533045/

Page 11 Photo by user tsapenkodg via Pixabay.com, https://pixabay.com/en/kittens-abyssinian-cat-2136803/

Page 27 Photo by user Leo_65 via Pixabay.com, https://pixabay.com/en/cat-breed-cat-abyssinian-close-fur-2392459/

Page 39 Photo by user skeeze via Pixabay.com, https://pixabay.com/en/abyssinian-cat-feline-egyptian-533921/

Page 47 Photo by user Bethany via Flickr.com, https://www.flickr.com/photos/vedder/11914463244/

Page 60 Photo by user editrx via Flickr.com, https://www.flickr.com/photos/windhaven/65402313/

Page 70 Photo by user Aleksander Markin via Flickr.com, https://www.flickr.com/photos/aviamarkin/12540460354/

Page 79 Photo by user Ref54 via Flickr.com,
https://www.flickr.com/photos/rfunnell/15560673944/

Page 89 Photo by user Taryn via Flickr.com,
https://www.flickr.com/photos/tarale/3431599998/

Page 102 Photo by user via Bethany Flickr.com,
https://www.flickr.com/photos/vedder/11914232194/

References

"Abyssinian" Cattime.com

<http://cattime.com/cat-breeds/abyssinian-cats#/slide/1>

"Abyssinian" A- Z Animals

<https://a-z-animals.com/animals/abyssinian/>

"Abyssinian Breed Standard" CFA.org

<http://cfa.org/Portals/0/documents/breeds/standards/abyssinian.pdf>

"Abyssinian Cat" Wikipedia.org

<https://en.wikipedia.org/wiki/Abyssinian_cat>

"Abyssinian Cat Breed" Petwave.com

http://www.petwave.com/Cats/Breeds/Abyssinian.aspx

"Abyssinian Cats Ideal Weight and Nutrition" Cat Mess

<http://catmess.blogspot.com/2009/12/cat-breeds-abyssinian-cat.html>

"Abyssinian Cat Information and Personality Traits" Hillspet.com

<http://www.hillspet.com/en/us/cat-breeds/Abyssinian>

"Basic Cat Training" LoveThatPet.com

<https://www.lovethatpet.com/cats/behaviour-and-training/cat-training-tips/>

"Breeding and Reproduction of Cats" MerckVetManual.com

<http://www.merckvetmanual.com/pethealth/cat_basics/routine_care_and_breeding_of_cats/breeding_and_reproduction_of_cats.html>

"Caring for Your Feline Companion" BrandonLakesAnimalHospital.com

<http://www.brandonlakesanimalhospital.com/client-resources/breed-info/Manx/>

"Cat Proofing Your House" HumaneSociety.org

<http://www.humanesociety.org/animals/cats/tips/cat_proofing_your_house.html?credit=web_id103701348>

"Cat Tips" HumaneSociety.org

<http://www.humanesociety.org/animals/cats/tips/>

"Cat Fanciers Glossary" Fanciers.com

<http://www.fanciers.com/other-faqs/gloss.html>

"Cat Glossary" Messybeast.com

<http://messybeast.com/cat-glossary.html>

"How to Train a Cat: Tips and Tricks" Purina.com.au

<http://www.purina.com.au/cats/training/train>

"Maintaining the Health of Your Abyssinian Using the Best Cat Foods" Catological.com

<http://www.catological.com/best-cat-food-abyssinian/>

"The Abyssinian Cat" Cat – Breeds – Encyclopedia.com

http://www.cat-breeds-encyclopedia.com/Abyssinian-cat.html

"The Decision to Breed" PetEducation.com

<http://www.peteducation.com/article.cfm>

"Tips for a Healthy Cat" Aspca.org

<https://www.petfinder.com/cats/cat-health/tips-healthy-cat/>

"Vaccines & Vaccination Schedule for Cats & Kittens" PetEducation.com

<http://www.peteducation.com/article.cfm>

"What do Abyssinians Eat?" Animal Care Tip
<http://animalcaretip.com/what-do-abyssinians-eat/>

Feeding Baby
Cynthia Cherry
978-1941070000

Axolotl
Lolly Brown
978-0989658430

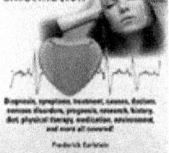

Dysautonomia, POTS
Syndrome
Frederick Earlstein
978-0989658485

Degenerative Disc
Disease Explained
Frederick Earlstein
978-0989658485

Sinusitis, Hay Fever,
Allergic Rhinitis Explained
Frederick Earlstein
978-1941070024

Wicca
Riley Star
978-1941070130

Zombie Apocalypse
Rex Cutty
978-1941070154

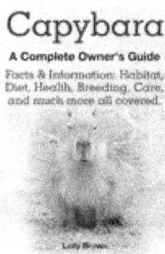

Capybara
Lolly Brown
978-1941070062

Eels As Pets
Lolly Brown
978-1941070167

Scabies and Lice Explained
Frederick Earlstein
978-1941070017

Saltwater Fish As Pets
Lolly Brown
978-0989658461

Torticollis Explained
Frederick Earlstein
978-1941070055

Kennel Cough
Lolly Brown
978-0989658409

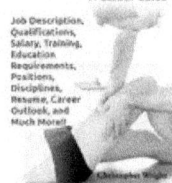

Physiotherapist, Physical
Therapist
Christopher Wright
978-0989658492

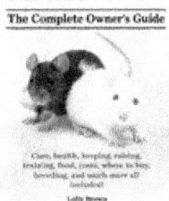

Rats, Mice, and Dormice
As Pets
Lolly Brown
978-1941070079

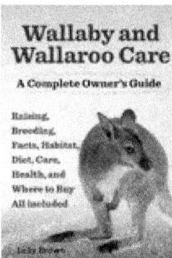

Wallaby and Wallaroo Care
Lolly Brown
978-1941070031

Bodybuilding Supplements
Explained
Jon Shelton
978-1941070239

Demonology
Riley Star
978-19401070314

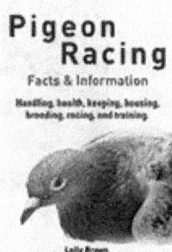

Pigeon Racing
Lolly Brown
978-1941070307

Dwarf Hamster
Lolly Brown
978-1941070390

Cryptozoology
Rex Cutty
978-1941070406

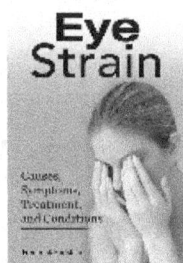

Eye Strain
Frederick Earlstein
978-1941070369

Inez The Miniature Elephant
Asher Ray
978-1941070353

Vampire Apocalypse
Rex Cutty
978-1941070321

www.ingramcontent.com/pod-product-compliance
Lightning Source LLC
LaVergne TN
LVHW051643080426
835511LV00016B/2460